10 WAYS TO USE LESS WATER

by Lisa Amstutz

PEBBLE
a capstone imprint

Published by Pebble, an imprint of Capstone
1710 Roe Crest Drive, North Mankato, Minnesota 56003
capstonepub.com

Copyright © 2024 by Capstone. All rights reserved. No part of this publication may be reproduced in whole or in part, or stored in a retrieval system, or transmitted in any form or by any means, electronic, mechanical, photocopying, recording, or otherwise, without written permission of the publisher.

Library of Congress Cataloging-in-Publication Data is available on the Library of Congress website.

ISBN: 9780756577964 (hardcover)
ISBN: 9780756578145 (paperback)
ISBN: 9780756578008 (ebook PDF)

Summary: Did you know that the average American home wastes 90 gallons of water a day? Help save water, money, and energy with these 10 simple steps and a hands-on activity. Find out what tips work for you and spread the word. Together, we can make a difference!

Editorial Credits
Editor: Mandy R. Robbins; Designer: Heidi Thompson; Media Researcher: Jo Miller; Production Specialist: Tori Abraham

Image Credits
Getty Images: JanuarySkyePhotography, Cover (bottom right), Kraig Scarbinsky, 16, Peter Dazeley, 18; Shutterstock: Aleksandra Suzi, 11, Alexander Knyazhinsky, Cover (bottom left), Bleshka, 9, Carlos Marques, 19, CGN089, 12, EpicStockMedia, 5, fizkes, 6, KAY4YK, 21, Monkey Business Images, 10, OlegDoroshin, Cover (top left), OlhaTsiplyar, 17, otsphoto, 13, pikselstock, Cover (top right), Pixel-Shot, 7, son Photo, 14, Stanislavskyi, 8, Yavdat, 15

All internet sites appearing in back matter were available and accurate when this book was sent to press.

Printed and bound in China. 5593

TABLE OF CONTENTS

Water Everywhere 4

How Do We Use Water? 6

Water Problems 8

10 Ways You Can Use Less Water 10

Activity: Track Your Water Use 20

    Glossary 22

    Read More 23

    Internet Sites 23

    Index 24

    About the Author 24

Words in **BOLD** are in the glossary.

WATER EVERYWHERE

Water is all around us. It fills rivers, lakes, and seas. It is underground. Water **vapor** is even in the clouds. Our bodies are mostly water too!

HOW DO WE USE WATER?

People need water to live. We drink it and wash with it. We brush our teeth with it. We use it to flush the toilet.

Water helps plants grow. House plants need water. Gardens and farms do too.

WATER PROBLEMS

Most of Earth's water is in the oceans. It is salty. It is not healthy to drink. Only a small part is **fresh water**. Without clean fresh water, humans can't survive.

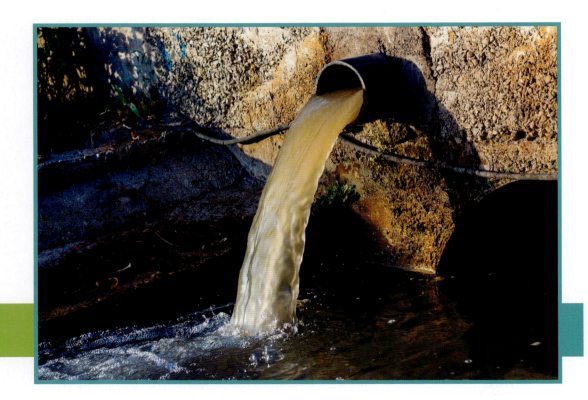

Sometimes people **pollute** water. They dump waste into it. Then it is not safe to drink. Other times, people use too much water. **Wells** and rivers run dry.

10 WAYS YOU CAN USE LESS WATER

1. Swish, swish. It's time to brush your teeth! Wet your brush. Then turn the water off until you are ready to rinse.

2. Do this when you wash your hands too. Don't let the **faucet** run while you scrub.

3. It's fun to take a bath. But a shower uses less water. Try to keep your showers short. Maybe you don't need one every day.

4. If you do take a bath, **reuse** the water. Scoop it out to water outdoor plants. Or wash your pet in it!

5. Toilets use lots of water. Ask your parents to put a full water bottle in the toilet tank. This will save water on each flush.

6. Laundry takes a lot of water. Ready to throw those pants in the wash? Wait! Can you wear them again? Hang up your bath towel to dry. Use it a few times before you wash it.

7. Washing dishes takes water too. Don't let the water run. Fill the sink. If you use a dishwasher, wait until it is full. Then run a load.

8. Do you get a new cup every time you get a drink? Keep a metal water bottle on hand to use fewer dishes.

9. Ugh, mud! Time to clean your bike! Don't let the hose run. Use a bucket of soapy water and a rag. Then spray off the soap at the end.

10. **Leaky** faucets can waste a lot of water. Tell your mom or dad if you spot one. See if they can stop the drip.

We can all do our part to save water. Can you think of more ways to help?

ACTIVITY: TRACK YOUR WATER USE

How much water do you use each day? Every time you use water, count how many seconds it runs. Write it down. Add it up at the end of the day. Then look for ways to use less each time.

GLOSSARY

faucet (FAW-suht)—an object with a valve that is used to control the flow of water; people use faucets to turn water on and off

fresh water (FRESH WAH-tuhr)—water that does not have salt; most ponds, rivers, lakes, and streams hold fresh water; oceans are saltwater

leaky (LEE-kee)—having a hole through which water can pass

pollute (puh-LOOT)—to make something dirty or unsafe

reuse (ree-YOOZ)—to use again, especially in a different way

vapor (VAY-pur)—a gas made from a liquid

well (WEL)—a deep hole from which you can draw water

READ MORE

DiOrio, Rana. *What Does It Mean to Be Green?* Naperville, IL: Little Pickle Press, 2021.

French, Jess. *Pedro Loves Saving the Planet.* Beverly, MA: Happy Yak, 2023.

Gleisner, Jenna Lee. *Let's Save Water!* Minneapolis: Jump!, 2019.

INTERNET SITES

How Can I Save Water?
youtube.com/watch?v=6yCAPAqXodc

Water Conservation Tips for Kids
thinkh2onow.com/water_conservation_tips_kids.php

Water Sense for Kids
epa.gov/watersense/watersense-kids

INDEX

bathing, 12, 13, 15
brushing teeth, 6, 10

drinking water, 6, 8, 9, 17

faucets, 11, 19
fresh water, 8

laundry, 15

plants, 7, 13
pollution, 9

toilets, 6, 14

washing dishes, 16

ABOUT THE AUTHOR

Lisa Amstutz is the author of more than 150 children's books on topics ranging from applesauce to zebra mussels. An ecologist by training, she enjoys sharing her love of nature with kids. Lisa lives on a small farm with her family.